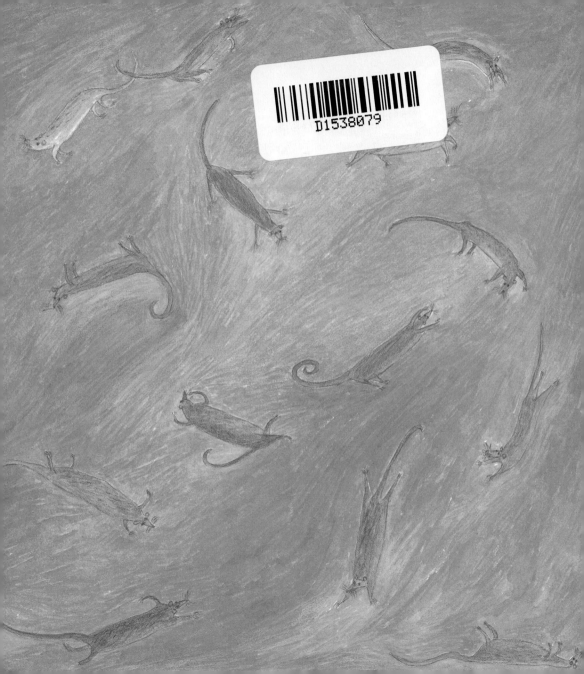

This edition published by Barnes & Noble, Inc.,
by arrangement with Michelle Lovric.
2000 Barnes & Noble Books
ISBN 0-7607-1991-8

10 9 8 7 6 5 4 3 2 1

Conceived and compiled by Michelle Lovric
Designed by Lisa Pentreath and Michelle Lovric
Illustrations Copyright © 2000 Lynne Curran
Compilation Copyright © 2000 Michelle Lovric

Manufactured in China by Imago

ehaving
adly

IF I WERE TO MAKE A CAT
BOOK IT WOULD SHOW THE
HORRIBLENESS OF CATS, THEIR
CRUELTY, THEIR JEALOUSY,
THEIR TERRITORIALITY,
THEIR UTTER LACK
OF FINE FEELING,
THEIR ABOMINABLE
SEX LIFE.

Germaine Greer (b. 1939)
Australian writer and feminist

God save all here,

except the cat.

Irish household greeting

Cats
behaving
badly

an anthology of
Feline Misdemeanors

compiled by Michelle Lovric   illustrated by Lynne Curran

BARNES
&NOBLE
BOOKS
NEW YORK

"O beautiful Fanchette,
your **bad behavior**
is so remarkably
becoming to you."

Sidonie-Gabrielle Colette (1873–1954)
French novelist

Every dog has his day, and a cat two Sundays.

English proverb

Contents

Shall I choke you, Cat, Or kiss you? Really I do not know.

Amy Lowell (1874–1925)
American poet

By Way of an

My Cat, Baggins

For I will consider my cat Baggins,
For he brings me morning gifts of fur and feather,
For he ignores my strident aversion to dawn corpses,
For he chants nightly in plainsong with next door's tom,
For he is equally tone-deaf and oblivious to hints,
For he scorns his cissy litter-tray,
For he banks his deposits among the seed-beds of neighbors,
For he waives this custom only in the interests of visitors,
For he fills my flat for their delectation with a lingering aroma,
For he shows concern for my spiritual welfare,
For he causes me to to lay up for myself treasures on earth,
For this he performs in ten degrees.

Introduction

For first he can recognize a cheap label with his eyes closed,
fasting reproachfully until I see his point of view,
For secondly he carries within him and without many small friends,
occasioning great expenditure on sprays, powders and pills,
For thirdly he rejects the emery of chestnut or cherry bark,
preferring the keener hone of woodchip or chair leg,
For fourthly he tests his pedicures on floor-length drapes,
developing a spaghetti-hoop effect of ruched weft,
For fifthly his taste inclines to a randomly-patterned carpet,
to which he practices projectile regurgitation,
For sixthly his favorite summer bed is the compost heap,
whereof he removes glutinous residue on my cream hearthrug,
For seventhly his favorite winter bed is mine,
on whose duvet he records details of his worst excursions,
For eighthly he is magnetically attracted to new manuscripts,
this force mysteriously waning when his feet are clean,
For ninthly he cares little about my decorative skills,
responding to my Christmas tree as Bonnington to Everest,
For tenthly his victories over local fauna seem somewhat pyrrhic,
promoting a general redistribution of resources from me to his vet.

For he appears to believe I should live on beans to keep him,
For he is probably right,
For this, his revision of my priorities, I am indebted,

Frequently.

Ann M. Foggatt
Contemporary English poet

Mad
about
Cats

A love of cats
is a vice of
inferior minds.

Alphonse Toussenel
19th-century French writer and sportsman

Listen, cats ladder your tight

8

Keeping cats is a mad practice, something like having children, but without that consciousness of public approval, of doing one's duty and of God being responsible. . .

from "The Contributors' Column" in *Atlantic Monthly,* 1922

To be female, single and the owner of one or two cats is acceptable. Just. Acquire a third cat, however, and your reputation disintegrates from mildly eccentric to certifiably mad.

Penny Wark
Contemporary English journalist

and so they must die!

Jenny Eclair
Contemporary English comedienne

"No! I cannot abide Cats," says the writer. "Pet Cats, wild Cats, Tom Cats, gib Cats, Persian Cats, Angora Cats, tortoiseshell Cats, tabby Cats, black Cats, Manx Cats, brindled Cats, mewing once, twice, or thrice, as the case may be, – none of these Cats delight me; they are associated in my mind with none but disagreeable objects and remembrances – old maids, witchcraft, dreadful sabbaths, with old women flying up the chimney upon broom-sticks, to drink hell-broth with the evil one, charms, incantations, sorceries, sucking children's breaths, stopping out late on the tiles, catterwauling and molrowing in the night season, prowling about the streets at unseasonable hours, and a variety of other things, too numerous and too unpleasant to mention."

A Cat-Hater quoted by
Charles H. Ross (1842(?)–97)
English writer

It is a solemn and well-known fact
that one of a million dogs gets a bad name,
while not one out of a million cats gets a good one.

Marvin R. Clark
19th-century American writer

Confound the cats! All cats – alway–
Cats of all colors, black, white, grey;
By night a nuisance and by day –
Confound the cats!

Orlando Dobbin
19th-century Irish writer

There is no man now living anywhere
Who hates cats with a deeper hate than I;
I hate their eyes, their heads, the way they stare,
And when I see one come, I turn and fly.

Pierre de Ronsard (1524–85)
French poet

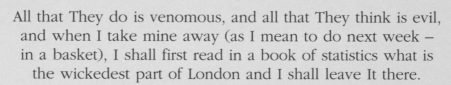

All that They do is venomous, and all that They think is evil,
and when I take mine away (as I mean to do next week –
in a basket), I shall first read in a book of statistics what is
the wickedest part of London and I shall leave It there.

Carl Van Vechten (1880–1964)
American writer and photographer

One of the most violent cat-haters of all time was a Chicago banker named Rockwell Sayre, who dreamed of ridding the world of cats by 1925, giving as his reasons that they are "filthy and useless," they "catch birds and spread disease," and that it is "toadying to depravity to keep a cat around the house." He gave small rewards to cat killers, ten cents each for the first 100, offered "$100 to the person who killed the last nasty cat on earth," had for his slogan,

"A catless world quick. . ."

Ida M. Mellen
20th-century American writer

I never meet a prowling cat without doing him the honor of shooting him.

Alphonse Toussenel
19th-century French writer and sportsman

Yet another anti-cat association! The formation of the Society for Promoting Cruelty to Cats is announced. In bidding a hearty welcome to the new-comer, which undoubtedly supplies a want, we would remark that one day a very large question will have to be tackled, namely, the desirability of combining all our hundred and one anti-cat societies into one vast organization. Personally, we are in favor of this. We are convinced that such an amalgamation would be able to sweep all cats off the face of the earth.

from *The Dog World and Anti-Cat Review,* written & illustrated by Dogs for Dogs
with the Assistance of Walter Emanuel, 1909

That cat! I wish she were dead!

Jane Welsh Carlyle (1801–66)
Wife of the Scottish historian Thomas Carlyle

As soon as they're o

The Cat Who Do

The cat **gives** the world **nothing** and **receives** from it **everything**.

Georgina Stickland Gates
20th-century American psychologist

Its reputation is detestable, the fact cannot be disguised,
and one must acknowledge that the cat does nothing to modify
the opinion in which it is held. It is entirely unpopular, but it
cares as little about this as it does about the Grand Turk.

Alexandre Dumas (1802–70)
French writer

Understand that your cat is a whore and can't help you.
She takes on love with the whiskery adjustments of a gold-digger.

Lorrie Moore
Contemporary American writer

12

...f your sight,
...ou are out of their mind.

...lter de la Mare (1873–1956)
English poet and novelist

...esn't Give a Damn

She uses you. She is a feckless,
disloyal creature, so proud of her
independence that she is quite
prepared to walk out forever on a whim –
or if someone makes her a better offer.

Richard Holliday
Contemporary English journalist

Cats. . .have cleverly developed the concept of
"treat 'em mean, keep 'em keen" to a fine art,
not to mention a life style.

Mira Bar-Hillel
Contemporary English journalist

Puss may look 'pon king, but him rader rat.
[a cat may look at a king, but would rather look at a rat.]

Jamaican proverb

13

When they watch me trotting to the shed,
those cats just see a huge tin of Whiskas on legs.
When I'm asleep, they see a huge tin of
Whiskas, with legs, lying on its side.

Lynne Truss
Contemporary English writer

But when a cat caresses you, it never looks at you.
Its heart seems to be in its back and paws, not its eyes.
It will rub itself against you, or pat you with velvet tufts, instead of talons;
but you may talk to it an hour together, yet not rightly catch its eye.

John Ruskin (1819–1900)
English writer, artist, designer and philosopher

Don't imagine that the cat is caressing you.
It is caressing itself.

Nicolas Sébastian Roch Chamfort (1741–94)
French writer

Why inquire too closely into the sincerity of her affection?

Philip Gilbert Hamerton (1834–94)
English writer

The cat is, above all things, a dramatist;
its life is lived in an endless romance though the drama is played out
on quite another stage than our own, and we only enter into it as
subordinate characters, as stage managers, or rather stage carpenters.

Margaret Benson
20th-century English writer

It is with the approach of winter that cats become in a special manner our friends and guests. It is then too that they wear their richest fur and assume an air of sumptuous and delightful opulence.

Pierre Loti (Louis Marie Julien) (1850–1923)
French naval officer and novelist

My cat in winter time usually sleeps upon my dog, who submits in patience; and I have often found her on horseback in the stable, not from any taste for equestrianism, but simply because a horse-cloth is a perpetual warmer when there is a living horse beneath it. She loves the dog and horse with the tender regard we have for foot-warmers and railway rugs during a journey in the depth of winter; nor have I ever been able to detect in her any worthier sentiment towards her master.

Philip Gilbert Hamerton (1834–94)
English writer

Cat love is always conditional.

Michelle Lovric
Contemporary English writer

He is very strong for he eats a great deal; he is an Eater of All Things. What are you eating? Give me some!

He is not beautiful, for he has no fur. Not having enough saliva, he has to wash himself with water. He miaows in a harsh voice and a great deal more than he need. Sometimes in his sleep he purrs.

Open the door for me!

I do not know why he has made himself Master; perhaps he has eaten something sublime.

He keeps my room clean for me.

In his paws he carries a sharp black claw and he scratches with it on white sheets of paper. That is the only game he plays. He sleeps at night instead of by day, he cannot see in the dark, he has no pleasures. He never thinks of blood, never dreams of hunting or fighting; he never sings songs of love.

Qu-ow

16

fraid of him.

Often at night when *I* can hear mysterious and magic voices, when I can see that the darkness is all alive, *he* sits at the table with bent head and goes on and on, scratching with his black claw on the white papers. Don't imagine that I am at all interested in you. I am only listening to the soft whispering of your claw. Sometimes the whispering is silent, the poor dull head does not know how to go on playing, and then I am sorry for him and I miaow softly in sweet and sharp discord. Then my Man picks me up and buries his hot face in my fur. At those times he divines for an instant a glimpse of a higher life, and he sighs with happiness and purrs something which can almost be understood.

But don't think that I am at all interested in you. You have warmed me, and now I will go out again and listen to the dark voices. **99**

Karel Čapek (1890–1938)
Czech journalist and writer

vow, quall, wawl, moon.

17

Anna Seward (1747–1809)
English poet

The Cat as Un

We may note that it is the only animal which has been tolerated, esteemed, and at times worshipped, without having a single distinctly valuable quality.

Nathaniel Southgate Shaler (1841–1906)
American writer

athomable Sphinx

Long dark grey fur
And Egypt in your eyes
Your Nile-green eyes
My kitten Cleopatra:
What Lion-mouse
Will fall beneath your paws
Your soft swift paws
My innocent Bubastis?

What Caesar sleeps
Surrendered to your guile
As you beguile
The Sun beyond the solstice?
Where sun meets moon
And night and day are one
All one to you
Enigma of all Sphinxes.

Jacintha Buddicom (1901–93)
English poet

There is no answer,
there is no answer to most questions about the cat.
She has kept herself wrapped in mystery for some 3,000
years, and there's no use trying to solve her now.

Virginia Roderick
20th-century American writer

We cannot of course, without becoming cats,
perfectly understand the cat-mind.

George Jackson Mivart (1827–1900)
English biologist

My cats are compromised.
I do not entirely trust them – they may be spies,
like dolphins, reporting to some unknown authority.

Jan Morris (b. 1926)
English writer

A cat walks about with a great purpose
dimly imagined in its brain.

Margaret Benson
20th-century English writer

It always gives me a shiver when I see a cat seeing what I can't see.

Eleanor Farjeon (1881–1965)
English writer

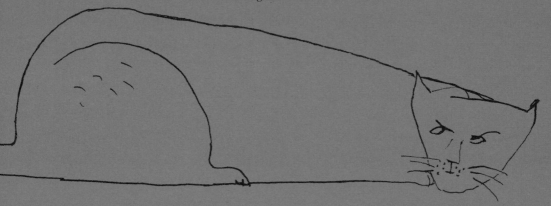

The cat remembers no past and anticipates no distant future. She is either half dozing or else absorbed in reacting to those things present to sense. She is feeling, perhaps dimly, sounds, sights, impulses, her own bodily condition. She is no philosopher, no mechanician, no student or critic of human affairs, merely a distant relative, poverty-stricken with respect to the most valuable of all possessions, but cherished for her air of aloofness and that aura of mystery which surrounds her.

Georgina Stickland Gates
20th-century American psychologist

The Insufferably

And while we treat cats like peopl

There is no pretense of sympathy about the cat.
He lives alone, aloft, sublime, in a wise passiveness.
He is excessively proud, and, when he is made the
subject of conversation, will cast one glance of scorn,
and leave the room in which personalities are bandied.

Andrew Lang (1844–1912)
Scottish man of letters

We strive in vain to break down his **sneering hostility**.

Clennel Wilkinson
20th-century English writer

High-Handed Cat

hey tend to treat us as if we were cats.

Jack Crossley
Contemporary English journalist

Cats dislike and despise us all. They take no trouble to conceal it. No woman is a heroine to her own tabby. No woman, it may be hazarded, is quite at her ease when writing a love letter under the eye of her cat. They have been known to turn the animal out of the room till the letter is finished.

Clennel Wilkinson
20th-century English writer

Some cats, as we all know, are born in full evening dress. White shirt, white tie. . .(whiskers). . .black tails and all. The illusion is perfect, particularly when they also have smart black paws to match. I love cats in evening dress; they wear it so much more elegantly than we do. Moreover, they never look incongruous in it.

Beverley Nichols (1898–1983)
English writer

A cat is a pygmy lion
who loves mice, hates dogs,
and patronizes human beings.

Oliver Herford (1863–1935)
English-born American humorist and writer

Every cat-owner must recall incidents in his experience which
in a moment have made up for the many humiliations he has
received at the hands of his cat – humiliations received as he
stood patiently while puss made an aggravatingly complete
pleripus of the room before she would deign to walk out of
the door, specially opened at her request; or as he fumed on
the front doorstep, on a raw November night, trying to induce
the priestess of the hearthrug to enter her abode, at his and
not her own good time and pleasure.

from *Cat and Bird Stories* from the *Spectator*, 1896

I lately heard, on good authority, of a case of a lady,
one of whose Cats came every morning to her bedroom door,
at six o'clock precisely, making so much noise mewing,
that it would awaken every one in the house, if she did not
hasten to get up, open the door, and shake hands with it,
after which ceremony it went quietly away.

Charles H. Ross (1842(?)–97)
English writer

You walk as a king scorning his subjects;
You flirt with me as a concubine in robes of silk.

Amy Lowell (1874–1925)
American poet

No Valentines from the cats again.
Sometimes I wonder whether they are
working as hard at this relationship as
I am. Few other pets, I imagine, were
lucky enough to find their Valentine's day
breakfasts laid out on heart-shaped trays,
with the words "From Guess Who" artfully
arranged in Kitbits around the edge. But
what do I get in return? Not even a single
rose. Not even a "Charming thought, dear.
Must rush." Just the usual unceremonious
leap through the cat-flap; the usual
glimpse of the flourished furry backside,
with its "Eat my shorts" connotation.

Lynne Truss
Contemporary English writer

Lulu, fluffy shape of night

How dare you Lulu, how dare you? I'm not my pet's animal.
Stop treating me so. . .
Stop acting the demonic fluffy totem I should obey. . .

You demolish my Napoleonic visions of being at last someone's Master,
Could you, at least, give me the chance of loving and caressing
in an absent-minded way, or a posh arrogant way, like a bloody 'real lady'?

Stop flattering yourself. . . you're not Cornelia Coastwood burnt in May 1643
we all know your next-door-alleyway background. . .

Mary Papastavrou (b. 1964)
Greek writer and playwright

"Speaking of cats," said Captain Foster, "I'm free to say that I don't like 'em. I don't care to be looked down on by any person, be he man or cat. . .Now I never knew a cat yet that didn't look down on me, same as cats do on everybody. A cat considers that men are just dirt under his or her paws. . ."

W. L. Alden
20th-century English writer

I have to endure the fierce contempt and sneering malice of Caruso, without any question the most ungenerous cat in Christendom. There is no doubt that he is a German at heart, and he rules us on the system of "frightfulness." There is a theory that the atrocious soul of Nietzsche has entered into him.

Sir Edmund Gosse (1849–1928)
English writer, poet and critic

While still a kitten, he absorbed the doctrine that it was only right and proper that degraded humans should forage for food, while he contributed to life little more than a decorative presence. Some philosophers have held that society is best organized on the basis of a slave class, and there is little doubt that Badger would subscribe to that view. Not unnaturally, he developed a touch of arrogance in his dealings with the lower orders: among whom he numbered, let us face it, practically every living thing except Badger.

Maurice Wiggin
20th-century English writer

I gave an order to a cat

I have seen a tabby with a black muzzle who,
for cold, calculated, yet perfectly well-bred
insolence, could have given points to a spiteful
duchess whose daughter-in-law "wasn't one of us,
you know." The heartless and deliberate rudeness
of that cat's behavior on occasion, had she been
a man, would have unquestionably justified
shooting at sight. The courtiers in the most slavish
palace of the East would have rebelled had they
received the treatment she meted out daily to those
who waited on her hand and foot. After a devoted
admirer had hunted breathless and bare-headed
over a large garden, and under a blazing July sun,
lest puss should lose her dinner, and had at last
brought her into the dining room in his arms, that
cat, instead of showing any gratitude, and instead
of running with pleasure to the plate prepared for
her, has been known to sit bolt upright at the
other end of the room, regarding the whole table
with a look of undisguised contempt, her eyes
superciliously half-shut, and a tiny speck of red
tongue protruding between her teeth. If the thing
had not been so exceedingly well done,
it would have been simply vulgar.

from *Cat and Bird Stories*
from the *Spectator,* 1896

...nd the cat gave it

My
cat
does
not
talk
as
respectfully
to
me
as
I
do
to its tail.
her.

Chinese proverb

Sidonie-Gabrielle Colette (1873–1954)
French novelist

A French writer says, the three animals
that waste most time over their toilet are
cats, flies, and women.

Charles H. Ross (1842(?)–97)
English writer

It has always struck me as extraordinary that cats are not permanently retained,
at high fees, in all schools for the training of mannequins and all
institutions where models are put through their paces. Before
each opening of the spring and autumn collections of Paris
the young women who are about to display the dresses
should be gathered together, and lined
up in a row, while pussy slowly
parades before them, to show
how it should be done.
True, the models would
probably all develop violent
inferiority complexes, for
the woman has yet to be
born who can manipulate
a train with the same grace
as pussy twitching her tail.
However, it would be worth
the risk.

In particular, pussy's technique
of entering a room should be
studied by all women who wish
to win friends and influence people.

Beverley Nichols (1898–1983)
English writer

You never coul

graceful or attractive...

or

...onvince a Cat that she was not pretty

Alfred Elwes (d. 1888)
English writer

29

Carlos condescended shortly to descend on his own account and to follow us from room to room, though always holding himself aloof. And when we had arranged our things and it was supper-time, and Carlos had indicated by a loud and unlooked-for miaow that attention to his well-being was necessary, we cut the very choicest morsels from our joint and confidently presented them. Carlos merely looked at the plate and turned his head aside. Then he looked again at us, as if to say, of course you will do better than this? On our pressing it again, he rose and walked a pace or so away, shaking his back paws as he did so, as if to rid himself of even the thought of contact with so poor a thing. Then he again looked at us expectantly, seeming to raise his brows a little over his beautiful emerald eyes. Completely subdued, we ran hither and thither. Would he like this? Would he try that? At last a tin of salmon was opened; and Carlos, having smelt it and retreated three times, at length, with the equivalent of a shrug of the shoulders, condescended to consume it, but slowly, and with every sign of an inward repulsion. When it was done, he turned his back on his plate and, shuddering a little, walked away and began very violently to wash himself.

This behavior continued for some time, Carlos always keeping us well in sight, but never permitting a caress; pouring scorn on our efforts to satisfy him with food or companionship. How to secure the approval of Carlos became a major problem of the day; how to produce food of the standard he thought adequate a no less important one. We made fantastic plans to win his trust: could we seem to save him, perhaps, from some dangerous dog? But there was no dog, we were soon to find, who did not go in mortal dread of Carlos.

Kathleen M. Abbott
20th-century English writer

30

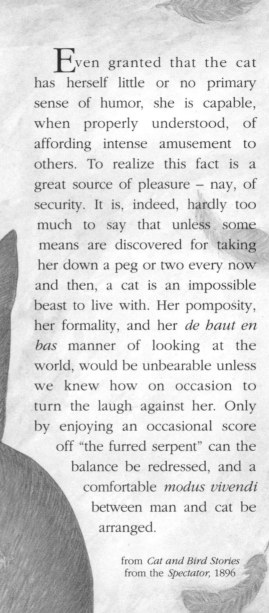

Even granted that the cat has herself little or no primary sense of humor, she is capable, when properly understood, of affording intense amusement to others. To realize this fact is a great source of pleasure – nay, of security. It is, indeed, hardly too much to say that unless some means are discovered for taking her down a peg or two every now and then, a cat is an impossible beast to live with. Her pomposity, her formality, and her *de haut en bas* manner of looking at the world, would be unbearable unless we knew how on occasion to turn the laugh against her. Only by enjoying an occasional score off "the furred serpent" can the balance be redressed, and a comfortable *modus vivendi* between man and cat be arranged.

from *Cat and Bird Stories* from the *Spectator*, 1896

The Cat as...

Cats find malicious amusement in doing what they know they are not wanted to do, and that with an affectation of innocence that materially aggravates their deliberate offense.

Helen M. Winslow
20th-century American writer

I lost a great part of my last hour for reading, yesterday evening, in keeping my kitten's tail out of the candles, – a useless beast, and still more useless tail – astonishing and inexplicable even to herself.

John Ruskin (1819–1900)
English writer, artist, designer and philosopher

Some cats should be tied up with strings,
They're always falling out of swings
Or else they're bumping into things.

Frederick White
20th-century English writer

Saboteur

In a cat's eyes,
all things
belong to
cats.

English proverb

All cats are keen gardeners, and in every
garden that I have ever made, their shadows lie across the path.
Sometimes, I must admit, the garden might have been made
more easily without their assistance. . . Like their owners,
cats soon decide which form of gardening most appeals to them –
though none of them, alas, ever takes any interest in weeding.
All of them, however, are keen waterers.

Beverley Nichols (1898–1983)
English writer

In any case, there is, at this moment, in our family, a sweet clinging vine of a
mother cat. . .She has any dog I ever saw beaten five ways for sheer, blind,
dumb, insistent Griselda affection for her folks. She loves us whenever she can
catch us, as we eat our meals, as we dress, as we sit to read or write. She licks
our hands and tickles us with her whiskers and looks up at us adoringly out of
her beautiful soft eyes; she loves us into spasms of nervous exasperation with
her (you must have seen that sort of cat) till we do brutal things to her, the brutal
things which people apparently enjoy doing to dogs, the impunity to do which
they praise dogs for granting. When we can stand for snuggling, purring,
molasses-like affection not an instant longer, we fling her off roughly, impatiently,
brutally, clear across the room as likely as not. Does Fauvette resent this? Not in
the least. She picks herself up patiently, lifts her pretty, gentle eyes to us once
more, and climbing laboriously up on us, prepares to love us some more.

Dorothy Canfield Fisher (1879–1958)
American writer

34

From kittenhood Mrs Muddle had been a very bad manager, or what is vulgarly called a *Muddler*. Her domestic concerns were often in a sad tangle, owing to her muddling ways. You might tell from the mere arrangement, or rather *dis*arrangement of the clover in her basket, that she had no organ of order; nor indeed was this to be wondered at. . .her great-grandmother was one of the notorious "three little kittens," who were so continually grieving their indulgent parent's heart by their disorderly ways, and whose reckless conduct in the repeated loss of their "mittens" has been celebrated in verse for the warning of others.

"E. L. H."
from *Captain Coddle's Catastrophe, and The Mishaps of Mrs Muddle:
both personages of Pussy Race*, 1872

She would, every morning after the piano was dusted, jump up upon the music-stool, and thence bound on to the keyboard. She would then walk about on it backwards and forwards, making the most abominable sounds – screeching notes, buzzing notes, groaning notes; groaning notes, buzzing notes, screeching notes, worse than the railway train.

William Swan Sonnenschein, afterwards Stallybrass
19th-century English writer

I have been told an amusing story about a well-known Doctor in Calcutta who had twenty cats, and kept a native servant whose exclusive business it was to make curry for them. On one occasion a lady with a strong antipathy to cats was expected to dinner, and so they were all shut up in a room at the top of the house. But by some accident the door was opened, and the twenty charged downstairs like a regiment of cavalry, whereupon, history relates, the lady fainted.

Mrs W. Chance
19th-century English writer

POEM FOR A CAT TO SIT ON

A cat sat on this poem when it
was only half-
written.

Although
poetry can often appear cold
and that, a sheet of
type-written paper must
seem warm to a cat.

But I don't mean
to suggest
that because this poem when only half-written
was sat on by a cat that it's in any way
diminished.

Because it is only a half-written poem sat on by a cat
about a poem sat on by a cat
when only half-written,

when I'd written only half of it,
I set it aside for a cat to sit on

and considered it finished.

Terry Egan
Contemporary Irish poet

Did the reader ever observe how very fond cats are of sitting on paper? One can hardly have a pet puss, and not observe this trait. If you have a book in your lap, up jumps Pussy, and seats herself right on top of it. If you are writing a letter, Pussy creeps along the table, singing so that you can hardly be angry with her, and places herself on the writing materials. My present puss prefers the *Daily Telegraph* to anything else for a bed at night, or to have her kittens on; indeed, if the *Standard* is lying on the same sofa, and she gets on to it by mistake, she will very soon get off, and on to the *Telegraph*.

William Gordon Stables (1840–1910)
Scottish writer

The cat has a habit . . . of being in a vast hurry to get out and yet, when the door is opened, standing on the sill deliberating so long that it is in danger of having its tail shut in. Why does it do this?

Ida M. Mellen
20th-century American writer

She had a great dislike to roast mutton cold, and when I had nothing else to offer her, her resentment was most marked: she refused my caresses, and walked straight off to my dressing-room, where on the top of the chest of drawers stood my bonnet-box. She jumped up and administered slaps to the box, until it fell on the floor, when she would come away at once, her revenge being gratified. This occurred on several occasions, and only when she was offered a cold mutton dinner. . .We quite looked out for it after the first few times, and would watch her walking off to my room, and then in a minute or two there would be "bump, bump," and my husband would say, "There goes your bonnet!"

anecdote quoted by William Gordon Stables (1840–1910)
Scottish writer

There were no cat skeletons found at Pompeii...obviously they screeched out of town at the first whiff of sulphur. "Tiddles!" they said in Pompeii. "Only you can save us!" But a flash of cat bum was all that was visible, as the volcano rumbled and split. Centuries later, when the site was excavated, many petrified human bodies were doubtless found in the attitude of surprised cat-owners calling to their pets in vain...Scrawled on a terracotta brick were some dying words in Latin, which, roughly translated, meant, "I don't believe it, the bloody cat has scarpered."

Lynne Truss
Contemporary English writer

38

Cats only
assume their
strangest,
most intriguing
and most
beautiful
postures
when it is
impossible to
photograph
them.
Cat calendars
always
disappoint
for they
only show
the public
range of cat
positions.

J. R. Coulson
Contemporary
English writer

"If I wanted to disturb the peace of this room, my good Dog, I should be clever enough to choose a chair with uneven legs to do my washing on, so that its feet would beat a regular "tick-tock, tick-tock, tick-tock" in time with the rhythm of my tongue. It's a method I've invented for obtaining my liberty. "Tick-tock, tick-tock" goes the chair. When She's reading or writing it soon gets on her nerves and She cries: "Be quiet, Kiki!" Knowing I'm within my rights I go on innocently washing. "Tick-tock, tick-tock." Maddened, She jumps up and opens the door wide for me. I go out very slowly, like one condemned to exile. When I'm outside I laugh to think how superior I am to all of them. "

Sidonie-Gabrielle Colette (1873–1954)
French novelist

"I like also to sharpen my claws on the corners of the oak chairs and the sofas. In another room, I like to go for an hour or so, by myself, and walk all over the bed-quilt, and leave the marks of my paws on it, it makes it more ornamental-looking. "

Carl Sartor
English writer
from *Sentimental Bobby, or The Autobiography of a Pussy Cat in Seven Mews*, 1898

"When I condescend to break some ornament with my royal paw, I give the impression that I'm chastising it. "

Sidonie-Gabrielle Colette (1873–1954)
French novelist

❝I hesitate to pass along this final instruction, since it is definitely not nice and is to be used only as a last resort. But there are some visitors who are too self-important or thick-headed, as well as hosts who are either too shy or too hospitable to discommode a guest, and hence won't ask them to move. You cannot afford to overlook this, or in any way to diminish or cast doubt upon the established fact that this is your chair from now until eternity, for you might not only undermine that position but many others. And so I do reveal that which has rarely been known to fail. You settle down quite quietly at their feet, paws tucked under, and make a smell. Before long the visitor will get up out of the chair and go over to the window, or cross to the other side of the room and take a seat on the sofa. At this point you get up on your property, wash a few licks as though nothing had happened, curl up, and relax. If your people smell it they will never let on, for that would be almost as though they had done it. **❞**

Paul Gallico (1897–1976)
American journalist and writer
from *The Silent Miaow: A Manual for Kittens, Strays, and Homeless Cats*

I have, of course, spent many a night in a cramped position to avoid disturbing a sleeping cat – or three – in the bed, although they would rearrange themselves and go back to sleep in a fraction of the time I spend lying awake contemplating my discomfort.

Mira Bar-Hillel
Contemporary English journalist

The Good-for Nothing Cat

The great charm of cats is their rampant egotism, their devil-may-care attitude toward responsibility, their disinclination to earn an honest dollar.

Robertson Davies (b. 1913)
Canadian writer and critic

Are cats lazy? Well, more power to them if they are.
Which one of us has not entertained the dream of doing
just as he likes, when and how he likes, and as much as he likes?

Fernand Méry
19th-century French writer

The best thing about cats is the way they make the business of being a cat look so darn easy. Hence catnap and catatonic. "It's been a hard day's night and I have been working like a cat?" You just never hear it said, do you?

Andrew Billen
Contemporary English journalist

Cats are intended to teach us
that not everything in nature has a function.

Garrison Keillor (b. 1942)
American writer

Our experimental evidence seems to show, as we have suggested,
a lack, or in any case a great dearth, of ideas or thoughts in the cat's mind.

Georgina Stickland Gates
20th-century American psychologist

He blinks upon the hearthrug,
And yawns in deep content,
Accepting all the comforts
That Providence has sent.

Alexander Gray
20th-century Scottish writer

Now when a cat decides to take his repose, he not only li...

I was singing to myself a bit, and talking to Pussy, who was almost
too comfortable to purr, only if I spoke she'd partly get up, and arch
herself very polite, and open her mouth to mew, and then be too
bone-idle to make any sound. But she looked at me as much as to
say, "I know you made this nice gledy fire to warm me, missus, and
I know you've got summat in larder for I, and thank you kindly."

Mary Webb (1881–1927)
English writer

own; he pours his body out on the floor like water.

William Lyon Phelps (1865–1943)
American educator, scholar and critic

The Cat as. . .

oolie = fur

purrieu = content

tut = limb

pro = nail or claw

Ignorant people think it's the noise which fighting cats make that is so aggravating, but it ain't so, it's the sickening grammar they use.

Mark Twain (Samuel Langhorne Clemens) (1835–1910)
American writer

Hardened Sinner

If cats had slime or scales instead of fur
there would be no gainsaying their utter nastiness.

Germaine Greer (b. 1939)
Australian writer and feminist

It is admitted that the dog has intelligence, a heart and perhaps
a soul, likewise it is agreed that the cat is a traitor, deceiver,
thief, an egotist, an ingrate.

Alexander Dumas (1802–70)
French writer

Women condemned to death for adultery are thrown into the Nile,
sewn up in a sack with a female cat. This refinement of cruelty is
perhaps due to the oriental idea that of all female animals the cat
bears the closest resemblance to womankind, in her suppleness,
her slyness, her coaxing ways, and her inconstancy.

M. Prisse d'Avennes
19th-century French Egyptologist

One strong characteristic attributed to the Cat
by its enemies and traducers is quarrelsomeness.

Marvin R. Clark
19th-century American writer

One is never sure, watching two cats washing each other,
whether it's affection, the taste or a trial run for the jugular.

Helen Thomson
Contemporary English writer

Marvin R. Clark
19th-century American writer

A cat is more intelligent than people believe,
and can be taught any crime.

Mark Twain (Samuel Langhorne Clemens) (1835–1910)
American writer

I could half persuade myself that the word felonious
is derived from the feline temper.

Robert Southey (1774–1843)
English poet

I regret to say that Pret has one fault. . .if he can steal anything
eatable, he will do so. Not because he is hungry, but merely for his
own amusement, does he scent out, steal, and hide something that
has been carefully concealed from him; just as youthful aristocrats
were, in former days, accustomed to steal door-knockers and bell-
handles, not for any pecuniary value which they might possess,
but simply as tangible proof of their nocturnal prowess.

The Reverend John George Wood (1827–89)
English naturalist and writer

Puss no tief, him shame.
[a cat would be ashamed not to be a thief.]

Jamaican proverb

The cat shuts its eyes while it steals the cream.

English proverb

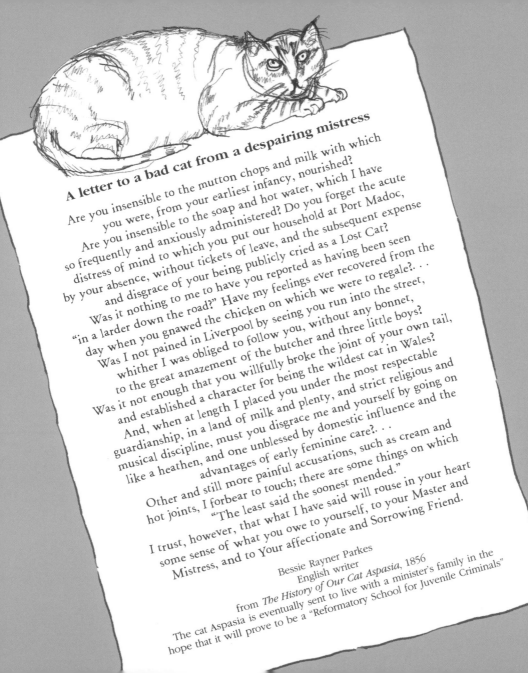

A letter to a bad cat from a despairing mistress

Are you insensible to the mutton chops and milk with which you were, from your earliest infancy, nourished?

Are you insensible to the soap and hot water, which I have so frequently and anxiously administered? Do you forget the acute distress of mind to which you put our household at Port Madoc, by your absence, without tickets of leave, and the subsequent expense and disgrace of your being publicly cried as a Lost Cat?

Was it nothing to me to have you reported as having been seen "in a larder down the road?" Have my feelings ever recovered from the day when you gnawed the chicken on which we were to regale?. . .

Was I not pained in Liverpool by seeing you run into the street, whither I was obliged to follow you, without any bonnet, to the great amazement of the butcher and three little boys?

Was it not enough that you willfully broke the joint of your own tail, and established a character for being the wildest cat in Wales?

And, when at length I placed you under the most respectable guardianship, in a land of milk and plenty, and strict religious and musical discipline, must you disgrace me and yourself by going on like a heathen, and one unblessed by domestic influence and the advantages of early feminine care?. . .

Other and still more painful accusations, such as cream and hot joints, I forbear to touch; there are some things on which "The least said the soonest mended."

I trust, however, that what I have said will rouse in your heart some sense of what you owe to yourself, to your Master and Mistress, and to Your affectionate and Sorrowing Friend.

Bessie Rayner Parkes
English writer
from *The History of Our Cat Aspasia*, 1856
The cat Aspasia is eventually sent to live with a minister's family in the hope that it will prove to be a "Reformatory School for Juvenile Criminals"

Cats sometimes hate as keenly as people. . . .
they too contrive their little revenges and Sicilian vendettas
whereby they may in some small degree compensate
for the insults doled out to their race.

Carl Van Vechten (1880–1964)
American writer and photographer

"I do not love a Cat," says a popular author, often quoted;
"his disposition is mean and suspicious. A friendship of years is
cancelled in a moment by an accidental tread on the tail. He spits, twirls
his tail of malignity, and shuns you, turning back as he goes off, a staring
vindictive face full of horrid oaths and unforgiveness, seeming to say,
'Perdition catch you! I hate you for ever.'"

Charles H. Ross (1842(?)–97)
English writer

A year or two ago, a man in the south of Ireland severely chastised his cat for
some misdemeanor, immediately after which the animal stole away, and was seen
no more. A few days subsequently, as this man was starting to go from home,
the Cat met and stood before him in a narrow path, with rather a wicked aspect.
Its owner slashed his handkerchief at her to frighten her out of the way, but the
Cat, undismayed, sprang at the hand, and held it with so ferocious a gripe, that
it was impossible to make it open its jaws, and the creature's body had actually
to be cut from the head, and the jaws afterwards to be severed, before the
mangled hand could be extricated. The man died from the injuries.

Charles H. Ross (1842(?)–97)
English writer

Yesterday was the fourth time Lenin visited since his arrival. I like talking with him. He is smart and educated and I like seeing his incredibly ugly face. Yesterday I also received a funny letter from Constantinople, which I have enclosed for you.

It is warm and balmy again, truly Spring time. Poor Mimi is making "Kuru" sounds. She impressed Lenin, who said that he had seen such a magnificent animal only in Siberia and called her a majestic cat. She even flirted with him, rolled on her back, and lured him to her. When he attempted to approach her, however, she hit him with her little paw and hissed **like a tiger.**

Rosa Luxemburg (1871–1919)
German left-wing revolutionary

The Cat as...

The disingenuity of character is betrayed by the obliquity
of their movements and the ambiguity of their looks.

Encyclopaedia Britannica, 1787

MONSIEUR PUSSY-CAT, BLACKMAILER

C'est un grand Monsieur Pussy-Cat
Who lives on the mat
Devant un feu énorme
And that is why he is so fat,
En effet il sait quelque chose
Et fait chanter son hôte,
Raison de plus pourquoi
He has such a glossy coat.
Ah ha, Monsieur Pussy-Cat
Si grand et si gras,
Take care you don't *pousser trop*
The one who gives you such *jolis plats.*

Stevie Smith (1902–1971)
English writer

Puss clearly trusts man; but she doesn't trust cats,
because she knows them better than we.

Karel Čapek (1890–1938)
Czech journalist and writer

Confidence

Trickster

" One of the most important things to learn for the proper and thorough subjugation of a household is attitudes. Attitudes, poses, expressions, play of body and features, all are lumped into the manner in which you remain continually and at all times alluring, inviting, enticing, seductive, fascinating, captivating, charming, winning, winsome, bewitching, enchanting, engaging, interesting, prepossessing. . . "

Paul Gallico (1897–1976)
American journalist
and writer
from *The Silent Miaow:
A Manual for Kittens,
Strays, and Homeless Cats*

If the cat is really cleverer than me, I just want to know one thing: why isn't he writing this article while I lie on top of the shed? But I suppose the answer is obvious when you put it like that. Cats are clever enough to get the better end of the symbiotic deal. "Tell you what," they say. "You write the piece, and I'll sit on it. You earn the money, and I'll eat the Friskies."

Lynne Truss
Contemporary English writer

Beware, my friend, of fiends and their grimaces;
Of little angels' wiles yet more beware thee;
Just such a one to kiss her did ensnare me,
But coming, I got wounds and not embraces.
Beware of black old cats, with evil faces;
Yet more, of kittens, white and soft be wary;
My sweetheart was just such a little fairy,
And yet she well-nigh scratched my heart to pieces.

Heinrich Heine (1797–1856)
German poet and essayist

Some boast that they have taught tricks to a cat; but the fact shows not so much that the cat was intelligent and docile as that its owners were.

Margaret Benson
20th-century English writer

Mostly, the way you define cat intelligence is by identifying the things they won't do.

Lynne Truss
Contemporary English writer

When his doting mistress was not looking, he managed to step off on that foot quite lively, especially if his mortal enemy, a disreputable black tramp, skulked across the yard. But let Thomas Erastus see a feminine eye gazing anxiously at him through an open window, and he immediately hobbled on three legs; then he would stop and sit down and assume so pathetic an expression of patient suffering that the mistress's heart would melt, and Thomas Erastus would find himself being borne into the house and placed on the softest sofa.

Helen M. Winslow
20th-century American writer

Coughing is part of the Act. It is usually employed if the fish is not served precisely to his liking. "Four" bends over the plate, sniffs, turns round, and then – always provided that he has an audience – goes straight into the Act with a positive Mimi of a cough. . .It is all very professionally timed and executed, and the only reason it is not quite heart-rending is that "Four", like many other Mimis whom one has seen expiring in Act Four of *La Bohème,* is exceedingly plump.

Beverley Nichols (1898–1983)
English writer

Not long ago I happened to be speaking in a somewhat admonitory tone to a "smoke" who lives in our neighborhood and who has succeeded in convincing two separate sets of people that she is their exclusive cat. I must say in all honesty that her reply put rather a new light upon the matter. She said, "But think of the pleasure I am able to give to two families instead of only one. I am therefore twice as valuable."

Paul Gallico (1897–1976)
American journalist and writer
from *The Silent Miaow: A Manual for Kittens, Strays, and Homeless Cats*

silent miaow

anticipatory purr

"I cannot begin to tell you
how effective the Silent Miaow can be for breaking down resistance,
always provided you don't overdo it but save it for the right moment.
The technique for this is ridiculously simple. You look up at the subject,
open your mouth as you would for a fully articulated miaow, such as you
emit if, say, you wish to leave the room and want the door opened,
or are hungry or irritated by something, except in this case you permit
no sound to issue. The effect is simply staggering.
The man or the woman appears to be shaken to the core, and will give
you practically anything. . .Even I, who have made a lifelong study of the
human species, am not able to tell you exactly why the Silent Miaow has this
devastating effect, or even the exact emotion it inspires in people.
The nearest I can come to it is that it creates a picture of helplessness
that the God syndrome is unable to resist. **"**

56

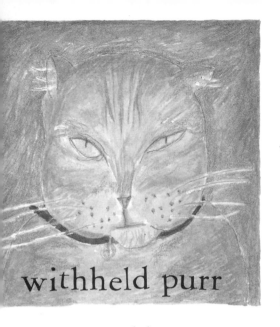

withheld purr

thankful purr

" Purrs fall into two classes:
the first, the Post-Appreciative or Thankful Purr, and the second,
the Anticipatory Purr. The Anticipatory Purr is a powerful stimulant if you want
some action, and when combined so as to follow immediately upon the
Silent Miaow, is practically irresistible.
Since the purr is accepted in every country of the world as indicative that you have
been pleasured, the Anticipatory Purr is most useful in jogging the conscience of a
human and making him or her feel guilty if he fails to come through. An advance
purr at meal-times or when cadging, or if they are packing up to go for a day in the
country and you'd like to go along too, makes it almost impossible for them to
refuse to gratify what you are already thanking them for . . . There is also an
important adjunct to this, namely the Withheld Purr, which is highly effective
if your people have transgressed and you are engaged in letting them know
that they have, and punishing them. **"**

Paul Gallico (1897–1976)
American journalist and writer
from *The Silent Miaow: A Manual for Kittens, Strays, and Homeless Cats*

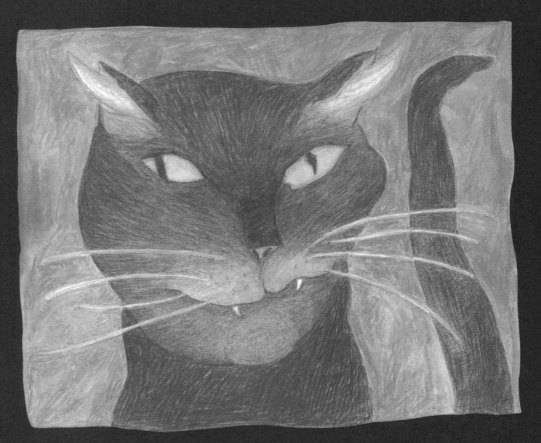

❝ I am the devil. Yes, the devil, that's what I said. You've only to look at me and you'll see there's no mistaking it. That's to say if you dare look at me! I'm black all over, a black scorched by the fires of hell. My eyes are poison-green, striated with brown, like the flowers of henbane. I've horns made of stiff white hairs springing out of my ears, and I fairly bristle with claws, hundreds and hundreds of 'em. As for my thin, restless tail, stuck on crooked, but lordly and most expressive, **there's only one word for it: diabolic. ❞**

Sidonie-Gabrielle Colette (1873–1954)
French novelist

The Dark Satanic Cat

I've heard my mother say that there ain't a cat mentioned in the whole Bible, from beginning to end. You just lay that to heart, and have nothing to do with cats.

W. L. Alden
20th-century English writer

The familiars of witches do most ordinarily appear in the shape of cats, which is an argument that the beast is dangerous to soul and body.

Edward Topsell (?–1638)
English religious writer

Black Cats and skulls have always been associated with magic and witchcraft, the most powerful weapon for spells being the skull of a black Cat that had been fed on human flesh.

Charles Platt
20th-century English writer

It was believed that the devil borrowed the black coat of the cat when he wanted to torment his victims; the large, fixed, green eyes of the animal had something to do with its terribly bad reputation.

Champfleury (Jules-François-Félix Husson) (1821–89)
French writer

At first everything I did made you laugh.
You laugh still, but I'm beginning to make you feel uneasy too. You laugh when I bring right up to you at meal-times a big cockchafer from the dunes, mottled like a plover's egg. But I crunch it up so ferociously, and pull the guts out of its fat stomach with such sickening greed, that you push aside your plate and let the soup grow cold. I unwind in graceful coils before you the entrails of the chicken you're going to eat later. And in the drawing-room I disdain the ribbon you hang from the door-latch and play instead with a beautiful live earth-worm, supple and elastic!
I eat everything, green flies and crabs, the dead sole on the sand and the live blind-worm which shines in the grass like a link from a steel chain. I kill the salamander on the rim of the fountain just to hear the exciting noise it makes as it suffocates. I lacerate the slimy skin of the toad with the points of my claws. I've sucked the milk of the grey cat, seizing the opportunity to bite her, and the milk of the collie bitch too, lying all huddled up with her huge woolly puppies. Ever since then her teats have been black. **"**

Sidonie-Gabrielle Colette (1873–1954)
French novelist

It is most certain that the breath and savor of cats
consume the radical humor and destroy the lungs,
and they who keep their cats with them in their
beds have the air corrupted and fall into
hectics and consumptions.

Edward Topsell (?–1638)
English religious writer

To dream of cats denotes much trouble and vexation;
to a lover, that your sweetheart is treacherous;
if you keep servants, that they are unfaithful
and will rob you.
A cat usually means an enemy.

Mother Shipton (1488–c.1560)
English witch

It is said that if you take
one of a Cat's nine lives,
it spends the next eight
haunting you to your doom. . .
So Beware! And tonight. . .
don't forget to put the Cat out.
Before if puts *you* out.

Michel Parry (b. 1947)
English writer

The Cat as..

" Thrown up through metal jaws, I enter my domain.
Blackbirds starlings pigeons sparrows voles
All are mine. Bones feathers beaks guts blood
All mine. For all life quartered here. I am death.

For aeons, nature blindly strove and groped
Towards the better mousetrap. Now I'm here.
I pounce, and grip a quaking gob of flesh
In my mouth, or my paw, or the other paw.

If I go through here, and past here, and up here,
Along this fence, and this one, and up this tree,
Here's the farthest outpost of my dominion.
I roost here, unchallenged. Squirrels can sod off.

Discordant tinny clangs and plaintive cries of "Puss!"
Mean dinner's served. Tail up, I saunter home
To "Sheba" beef and liver, tripe or heart.
Milk's for my staff; they serve me all the cream.

Replete and sleek, the pleasures of the flesh
Come next. Compliant fingers stroke my purring fur.
And then the airing cupboard's womb of winceyette
Enwraps my warm siesta. This is the life!

I am going to keep writing like this. "

Bob Newman (b. 1953)
English poet and parodist

62

Serial Killer

The nest is empty, and silent and lone;
Where are the four little robins gone?. . .

But you need not try
to look good and wise:
I see little robins, old
puss, in your eyes. . .

Gail Hamilton
(Mary Abigail Dodge)
(1838–96)
American essayist

A nightingale begins to sing;
suddenly the music is mute –
both the nightingale and song
have fallen into the jaws of the cat.

Champfleury (Jules-François-Félix Husson) (1821–89)
French writer

You know a hunting cat by its whiskers.

Bengali Proverb

63

The

cat

does

not

negotiate

with

the

mouse.

Robert K. Massie
(b. 1929)
English writer

A
mouse
in
the
paws
is
worth
two
in
the
pantry.

Louis Wain (1860–1939)
English artist

The cat weeps over the death of the rat, but it is false sympathy.

Chinese proverb

It was in the city house that Pret invented his novel and unique method of killing mice. . .Taking the unfortunate victim by the tip of its tail, he used to convey it to the top of the house, and when he had got to the uppermost landing he would push his head between the banisters and deliberately drop the mouse through the well, cocking his ears forward to catch the sound of the fall. As soon as he heard the thump of the mouse's body against the hall floor, he would cry "Wow!" in a very triumphant tone, and dart downstairs, with his tail erect, to recover his prey. . .He would then amuse himself with it for an hour or two, and finish by biting off its head, and leaving both the head and the decapitated body at the door of my room.

The Reverend John George Wood (1827–89)
English naturalist and writer

Tabby the rake came home now over the roofs. All night long he had roamed through lonely barns and dispersed legions of rats. Their blood had drenched his sharp armed jaws and drunk with victory, he had sported and rolled on the heaps of the slain.

F. W. Zachariae
German writer
from *Tabby in Elysium*, 1781, translated from the German by R. E. Raspe, creator of Baron Munchausen. Tabby is killed when he attacks his mistress's parrot. His soul hastens to Hell, but he returns to haunt his earthly family until they give him a decent burial.

Guilt is not known in the world of cats.

Michelle Lovric
Contemporary English writer

The Cat as . . .

Most cats like succotash, macaroni, noodles, peas, parsnips, squash, bread, cake, cereals, puddings, and other starchy food. Asparagus is believed to be the favorite vegetable of nearly all cats. They also favor cucumber, eggplant and celery, raw carrots, beets; and some like onions, as well as melons, nuts, coconut, raisins, lemon peel, dates, figs, olives, and grapes. . .They are fond of greens, lettuce, catnip, verbena, valerian, patchouli, lavender, grass, beach grass, umbrella grass, Californian bluebell, and the silver vine. The silver vine is eaten entire – root, branch, stem and leaf.

Dairy products are eagerly accepted – eggs, butter, cheese, and milk in every form, including ice cream, junket, and custard. Other beverages taken are tea, coffee, tomato juice, fruit juices, broths and alcoholic liquors.

Ida M. Mellen
20th-century American writer

The poor Cat had a dreadful pain in his stomach, and could eat only thirty-five mullet in tomato sauce, and four helpings of tripe garnished with Parmesan cheese. Because he thought the tripe was a bit tasteless, he asked three times for more butter and more grated cheese!

Carlo Collodi (Carlo Lorenzini) (1826–90)
Italian writer

A cat isn't fussy – just so long as you remember he likes his milk in the shallow, rose-patterned saucer and his fish on the blue plate. From which he will take it, and eat it off the floor.

Arthur Bridges
Contemporary writer and humorist

Gourmand

aliloo = water   bl = meat

milk = ter   pool = roller

ptleo-bl = mouse meat

bleeme-bl = cooked meat

Marvin R. Clark
19th-century
American writer

Cats have an extra organ that we do not have. . . Thanks to the Jacobsen organ, a cat will know if its food has gone stale long before reaching its bowl.

Jack Crossley
Contemporary English journalist

Puss eat ratta till him say ratta tail 'tink.
[the cat eats the rat but leaves the tail, saying it stinks.]

Jamaican proverb

El gato g'avea un campo, e per un pesse el l'ha vendù.
[the cat used to have a field, but he sold it for a fish.]

Venetian proverb

When puss hab money him buy cheese.

Jamaican proverb

" Let us say they have put down a dish of food of some sort for you and are benignly standing by in their self-appointed roles of Givers of Good Things. Go up to it, take a good sniff or two at it, poking your nose all in and around the dish as though trying to find one single palatable article in it, perhaps even a taste of one. Then look them full in the face for a moment. No cries of any kind are necessary; your expression will say unmistakably, Surely you can't mean you expect me to eat this? Walk away. "

Paul Gallico (1897–1976)
American journalist and writer
from *The Silent Miaow: A Manual for Kittens, Strays, and Homeless Cats*

68

You can feed a cat until he bulges; if he is one of my cats he will use up his expensive calories by hunting twice as hard. My cats try to eat most of the things they catch and are frequently forced to regurgitate long cylinders of fur, eyes, guts and teeth. Then they leap into my lap and kiss my nose, endowing me with a fishy blast of cannibal breath as a sign of their deep attachment.

Germaine Greer (b. 1939)
Australian writer and feminist

. . . my siamese, Samantha, was such a pain in the tail I frequently wondered if life would not be better if she were to get enteritis like other cats and go to cat heaven. From babyhood she ate like a ninety-year-old dowager duchess. *Forget* cat food – she wouldn't touch liver, tuna, ground sirloin, and what she *did* eat had to be just *born* – one day in the frig was too old!

Helen Gurley Brown (b. 1922)
American writer

There is something else working for you in this game, and that is your snob value as an eccentric individualist for dining-out conversation, in which they are able to take part in bragging matches such as: "Our cat will eat only *moules farcie* sprinkled with cashew nuts." "Ho, ho, you think that's a funny one. Our kitty will eat nothing but Alaska king crab claws, stewed lightly in Czechoslovakian butter, served on a bed of French anchovy toast." The more complicated a dish you can work out in order that your people may come out on top in such ploys, the more grateful they will be to you in the end. . . "

Paul Gallico (1897–1976)
American journalist and writer
from *The Silent Miaow: A Manual for Kittens, Strays, and Homeless Cats*

69

The Cat as . . .

Knit

my

dog

a

pair

of

breeches

and

my

cat

a

codpiece.

English proverb

BLACK DESIGNS

"It's that time of year, and they won't let me out
Celandines, brimstones and chasing my tail
I know what they're planning, what this is about –
They've found me a husband, a pedigree male.

His name is Fernando Fitzwilliam the Third,
He's a gold-plated tom, he's the right sort of stuff
But not of *my* choosing; he sounds like a nerd
When what turns me on is a nice bit of rough.

Satan is out there, I smelt him today
He's a cat with machismo, a cat with a past,
A charmer, a tough nut, a no-good, a stray,
Fernando Fitzwilliam, you're simply outclassed.

The scullery window's a technical breeze
I lift up the catch with my paw from below
Then out through the casement, a sinuous squeeze
I'll return before morning and no one will know.

Fernando Fitzwilliam is duly presented,
A toff with a candyfloss marmalade coat
I give him the brush-off, but then I consent – it
Is like being jumped by a short-sighted stoat.

They're feeding me chicken and spooning me cream,
I'm lying on velvet, they're stroking my back
They're banking on winners, I'm letting them dream
For the kittens I bear will be totally black."

Elizabeth Kay (b. 1949)
English/Polish writer

70

Casanova

The strength of their sexual feelings
is notorious.

George Jackson Mivart (1827–1900)
English biologist

One may not, on the printed page, be as forthright
as the cat is on the living-room carpet. . .

Frances and Richard Lockridge
Contemporary American writers

In his soul he is a dramatist,
an artist in sensation.

Margaret Benson
20th-century English writer

The female is remarkably salacious; a piteous, squalling,
jarring lover. Its eyes shine in the night: its hair when
rubbed in the dark emits fire; it is even proverbially
tenacious of life: always lights on its feet: is fond of
perfumes, *marum,* cat-mint, valerian, etc.

Thomas Pennant (1726–98)
English zoologist

The black cat in the wildest state of spring lust careers
about the garden after Ralph, crying out to be raped.

Dora Carrington (1893–1932)
English painter

The

she-cat

who

has

a

tom-cat

puts

on

airs

Creole proverb

71

"Furry," I cried, "do you think this is wise?. . ."
But the moment was charged for him with emotion too deep. I put out my hand and touched his fur and he briefly acknowledged my sympathy. There was nothing to do but to leave him there and continue the reading of our book.

A short time of silence intervened; I began to hope she had gone away. But my voice was cut in a period elegant as a Queen Anne house by a deep, full-throated, primitive cry. It put to flight the peace of the night. War to the death, or passion so wild it was scarcely distinguishable from it, trembled within its intensity. Civilization fell away; we were carried centuries back in time; naked and dark and elemental, it rose and savagely rent the air. We looked at each other and lowered our eyes. Cry after cry came like the wind. A shifting perspective within the sound suggested movement at rates incalculable; the movement itself was a silent thing. Urgency rose, and expectation; a growing crescendo within desire preluded some frightful consummation. In love or in death the wave must break. It did, with a frightful hissing sound. Silence returned; peace returned. A sense of achievement was in the night. It rested. Moonlight fell into the room. The leaves of the little apple tree began to tap once more on the panes.

We finished the chapter; we thought of coffee. The firelight danced on the shining walls as I rose and crossed the room to the door. Expecting nothing, I lifted the latch. And just outside, on the polished floor, sat a small white triangle of cat. He sat up, though his paws were wide apart, suggesting a state that approached collapse; the pose was philosophical, dashed with a look such as Eve must have worn on her first bite into the apple. The eyes that he raised were full of experience. Knowledge passed rapidly between us.

"You see, it has happened," he seemed to say.
"But how extraordinary!" said the eyes.

They explored the deep places of strangeness. At last, with a comical upward look, in which only the whites of them could be seen, *"Mais c'est la vie,"* he finished, and fell sideways. He fell in the shape in which he sat, abandoning sense so suddenly he could not collect himself for the fall. The impact of life had been too strong. Our delicate furry thing had fainted.

Kathleen M. Abbott
20th-century English writer

Tom remained true to his marriage vows for a long time, but one day, about six months after his advent in the household, he was missing, and the neighborhood was searched for Tom. He remained away until the following afternoon, when he returned, looking sheepish, while his appearance bore unmistakable evidence of his having been indulging in a debauch.

Marvin R. Clark
19th-century American writer

GRATEFULLY ACKNOWLEDGED

Every effort has been made to trace the copyright-holders of the material included in this book. In the event of any unwilling or inadvertent use of uncleared material, or for omitting the correct notification, the editor apologizes, and would be grateful to hear from the copyright-holder, and undertakes to amend any subsequent edition accordingly. The editors gratefully acknowledge permission of the following sources to use copyrighted material in this book: extracts from *Cat-enchanted* by Kathleen M. Abbott, first published by Frederick Muller in 1950. "Blue Persian" from *Cat Poems* by Jacintha Buddicom, published by Leslie Frewin Publishers Ltd. Copyright © 1973 Jacintha Buddicom. extracts from *Intimate Things* by Karel Čapek, published by George Allen and Unwin, now Unwin Hyman, an imprint of HarperCollins Publishers Ltd. Copyright © 1935 Karel Čapek. extracts from "White" in *Other Creatures*, "She is Ill" in *Creature Conversations* and "The Tom-Cat" and "Poum" from *Creature Comfort* by Colette, translated by Enid McLeod from the *Fleuron* edition, oeuvres complètes de Colette de l'Academie Goncourt (1949) and published as *Creatures Great and Small* (1951) by Martin Secker & Warburg, Ltd. extracts from the article "Little pet with the lion heart" by Jack Crossley from *The Times* on November 8th, 1997 reviewing the book *The Complete Feline Problem Solver* by Roger Tabor, published by David & Charles. Copyright © 1997 Jack Crossley/Times Newspapers Ltd. "Poem for a Cat to Sit on" by Terry Egan is reprinted by permission of the author. Copyright © 2000 Terry Egan. extract from "Why I like cats more than dogs" by Dorothy Canfield Fisher, reprinted by permission of Vivian S. Hixson, on behalf of Dr John Paul Scott. "My Cat, Baggins" by Ann M. Foggatt, first published in *Catatonic 2* in 1991. Copyright © 1991 Ann M. Foggatt. extracts from *The Silent Miaow: A Manual for Kittens, Strays and Homeless Cats* by Paul Gallico. Copyright © 1964 Paul Gallico. Reprinted by permission of Crown Publishers, Inc. extracts from "Confessions of a Cat Addict" by Germaine Greer, published in the *Oldie*, on September 3rd, 1993. Copyright © 1993 Germaine Greer. Reprinted by permission of Gillon Aitken Associates Ltd on behalf of the author. extract from *Having It All* by Helen Gurley Brown. Copyright © 1982 Helen Gurley Brown. Reprinted by permission of Simon & Schuster. extracts from articles by Richard Holliday, Mira Bar-Hillel and Andrew Billen reprinted by permission of Solo Syndication Limited. extract from *Cats Company* by Michael Joseph, first published by Geoffrey Bles in 1930. "Black Designs" by Elizabeth Kay is reprinted by permission of the author. Copyright © 2000 Elizabeth Kay. extract of letter by Rosa Luxemburg from *The Letters of Rosa Luxemburg*, edited and with an introduction by Stephen Eric Bronner, published by Humanities Press International, Inc. Copyright © 1978 Stephen Eric Bronner. extracts from *The Science and Mystery of the Cat* by Ida M. Mellen, published by Charles Scribner's Sons, a division of Simon & Schuster. Copyright © 1940 Charles Scribner's Sons; Copyright renewed © 1968 Ida M. Mellen. extract from *Self-Help* by Lorrie Moore, first published by Alfred A. Knopf 1985. Copyright © 1985 M. L. Moore. "Cat" by Bob Newman is reprinted by permission of the author. Copyright © 2000 Bob Newman. extracts from *The Cats ABC* and *Cats XYZ* by Beverley Nichols, first published by Jonathan Cape in 1960 and 1961 respectively. Copyright © 1960 and 1961 Beverley Nichols. Reprinted by permission of Eric Glass Ltd. extract from "Lulu, fluffy shape of the night" by Mary Papastavrou is reprinted by permission of the author. Copyright © 2000 Mary Papastavrou. extract from the introduction to *Beware of the Cat, Weird Tales about Cats*, edited by Michel Parry, published by Taplinger Books and Victor Gollancz Ltd. Copyright © 1972 Michel Parry. "Monsieur Pussy-Cat, Blackmailer" from *Two in One* by Stevie Smith, first published by Longman in 1971. Copyright © 1962, 1966 Stevie Smith. Reprinted by permission of James MacGibbon. extracts from *Making the Cat Laugh* by Lynne Truss. Copyright © 1995 Lynne Truss. Reprinted by permission of Hamish Hamilton. extract from article by Penny Wark, published in *The Sunday Times* on February 2nd, 1997 is reprinted by permission of News International Syndication. extracts from *Life with Badger* by Maurice Wiggin, first published by John Baker Publishers Ltd. Copyright © 1967 Maurice Wiggin.

The Artist would like to thank Susan McDowall at Townhead Farm Cat Rescue, Gifford, East Lothian, for the supply of raw material, and endless kindness towards badly behaved cats, and towards cats who have suffered bad behavior. The Artist would also like to thank the following people, whose pictures appear in this book: Jetta Brown, Tim and Sarah Chalk, Raymond Honeyman Paul and Yvette Spencer, Sue Stockwell, Michael Swift.